LIVE LIKE A KING

By: Benyamin. K.B

Book Name: LIVE LIKE A KING
Author: BENYAMIN.K.B
Publisher: SUPREME CENTURY
www.supremecentury.com
ISBN:978-1939123725
Cover Designer:Ghazal Mirzaei
Author's contact:benyaminkb76@yahoo.com
Publication date:June 26,2018

LIVE LIKE A KING

Secrets to have a luxury   life .
Never mind how much is your income .
Benyamin. K.B

Table of content

Introduction

You may have read many books, for example says:
How can you be billionaire?
How can you have the biggest business?
How can you have a good life?
How can you be a good parent?
How can you enjoy your life?
How can you be the best manager?
If you Look at these books, you can see that the writer at first destroys your inner feelings. The writer says that you don't have any self-confidence, you are not a good parent, you are poor and you don't have your ideals.
They suggest you to find the better life somewhere. They say that a good life is somewhere in future.
They destroy you and they want to make you a new person. They don't know that you don't have enough time to change all your life, vision and character in a long time program.
In this book, I will tell you how you can have a perfect life immediately.

You should not gain something in the future to have a better , perfect and luxuary life.

You have these entire elements for a perfect life in yourself just now.

I will tell you how you can have a perfect life.

Just read this book like a newspaper.

I suggest you to read this book several times. Each time you will gain a new thing and you will pick up a precious thing.

The last secret of a perfect life

When a person comes to this world, he is not aware of being in this world. He is like a baby animal but I say even weaken than a baby animal.

He doesn't know where he is and what a long way for living is in front of his life.

So, before you start a perfect life, you should be familliar with some elements which stick to your every day acts.

Five Senses

If you see and have a more attention to people's life, you can see the most of this people are trying to satisfy their five senses.

They go at work to gain money, to buy different kinds of fruits, to enjoy their tastes or they buy different foods in the same reason just to test more different tastes in order to have more things for enjoyment.

They go at work for more money in order to satisfy their sight sense by going to journey or buying a big size TV.

They go to beautiful beaches and lay on the warm and soft sands and buy a luxury bed to satisfy their sense of feeling, as we can put sexual enjoyment in this category.

They gain and pay money to buy their favorite music or go to a far beautiful place to hear the voice and song of the animals and birds to satisfy the sense of hearing.

Sometimes they spend much more money to buy their favorite

perfume, flowers or spicy foods to satisfy their sense of smelling. When you lived fully in your five senses, your desires and wills will be changed. it's the time for suicide. Some people in this position kill their body because they think that there is not anything to be enjoyed by their five senses.

They have tasted everything. They have eaten and tasted everything which had the ability of being eaten, so there is not anything to satisfy him or her. This rule of dissatisfaction is the same for all other senses as seeing, hearing, touching and smelling.

Some people do suicide in a different way. They don't kill their body; they kill something beyond the body. They say: we don't want to kill our body but we want to continue our life by enjoyment, but when I don't enjoy by eating or drinking and when I don't enjoy by going to travel, by buying beautiful house or car, by sex and etc, what should I do to not be depressed and be able to continue my ordinary life?

When a person comes to this situation, it is very critical. It's the time to be a different person. It's the time to launch as a shuttle. It's the time that everything is going to have a different value than they had until now.

It's the time for a great jumping. It's the time to be a

different perfect man.

When five senses never satisfy you and you rejected the suicide, you are entering to a new situation. In this situation you will not kill your body; you will kill your desires which are connected to your five senses.

A birth will happen in this time. It is your real birthday. You will live in a different way; you will look at things in a different ways.

If a delicious food don't satisfy you and you don't enjoy it, certainly giving this food to a hungry person will satisfy you and you will enjoy from this action. You will feel like a drunken person for days.

Nobody can be perfect without experiencing this five senses. If you or one of your family members especially your children want to be a perfect man or woman and if you want to have a successful family, you should experience your five senses fully. You should live with your five senses as completely as you can.

If you want to be a great man or woman in every field in your life, you should be mixed in your five senses.

You may ask how I can be mixed with my five senses and what the relation is between living with five senses and being a perfect man and more of all, have a perfect life?

Some people could change their ordinary life into a perfect and even royal life just in one day and some people after months and some of them never could change it till now.

One is equal to thousand

This is the greatest rule in five senses.
You may ask what it means and how one can be equal to thousand?
I ask you a question. If you drink a glass of milk, is there any different between second or third glass in taste? What about thousandth?
If you eat one beef stake, is there any different between the stakes that you have eaten before or you will eat tomorrow? It is obvious that the next glasses of milk or more stakes are not different and we know that the second one is not more delicious and the thousandth is not the most delicious one. I want to say that if you eat or drink any thing one time, it is the same as you have ate it thousands time. This rule can be true for all five senses. If you see jungle, sea, beautifull villages, beautifull flowers, moon or etc, several times, all of them can be the same if you want to enjoy by your sight sense. A red rose will never be more red if you watch it several times.
If you drunk a cup of tea yesterday, its taste will be

the same tea of today and tomorrow.

If you like one song more than other songs, you can not hear more words than before.

Sleeping in a soft bed will give you the same feeling of sleeping several times on it.

Even sex has the same feeling in first, tenth or thousandth time in your life.

So we can see that, those senses which are known as five senses like sense of sight, hearing, tasting, feeling and smelling, if have been used for enjoyment by a person, the quality of this enjoyment is the same in his whole life time.

So, according to this idea we can mention that one is equal to thousand.

I have a suggestion:

If you remember your life and memories, you can find that when you were doing something you were imaging something else.

You may ask, what do you mean?

For example, when you were drinking a glass of orange juice, you may were thinking about the conversation or strugle which you had with your friend or parents.

You were thinking about every thing but, you didn't have attention to your orang juice.

You may drunk hundreds of glasses of orange juice in your life till now but you never focused on the taste of it from the beginning to the end.

When you are going to drink anything, for example tea, juices or any kind of drinks, have a complete attention to it, attention to its taste.

Is it sweet or soure or does it have other tastes? Is it warm or cold? What color is it? So focouse your all senses on it. Don't think about any things but your drinking. If you focous your all senses on it, you will completely feel it and if some day ask yourself for example how is the taste of a cup of tea or coffee, you can remember and feel its taste by all of your body's cells.

I have a suggestion:

You can do what I said about drinking, by foods. You can taste all kinds of foods that you eat from the morning as a breakfast or lunch and supper. Focuse on their tastes.

Concentrate your all five senses on their tastes.

Remember if it is warm, soft, hard, cranchy or any special quality which they have and you didn't have any attention to them till now.

I have a suggestion:

When you are wearing your Shirt, dress or shoes, have an attention to their quality as if they are soft, warm or if they give you any kind of feeling which you never felt befor. Attention to their color and try to find how is your feeling when you wear a cotton shirt or wollen coat or sport shoes?

When you wear different clothes focouse your five senses on it. Specially try to know what is your feeling when it touches your skin.

When you go to take a shower or when you go to a pool, focous your sense on the water which touches your body. What do you feel when the water touches your body? What do you feel when the water comes out from the shower and touches your body?

Try to feel its coolness, warmness and softness.

When you go into the pool, try to concentrate and focous on the feelings that you have when your body touches the water.

You may went to pool severd times or tooke a shower too many times but you were thinking about everthings except the shower or swimming and the feelings which the water gives you during that time.

I have a suggestion:

When you are in the bed with your partner, try to have a great attention to your all actions. Have attention to the kisses one by one, be aware of your hands when any times you touch his or her body.

Be aware of taking off the clothes and second by second be aware of the softness and warmness of your partner's body. Even attention to the rhythm of her or his breathes. Focous on the feeling when you touch your partner's body by your body.

Try to remember the end of your sexual relation when you are going to be satisfy after too many kissing and touching. If you have another sex tomorrow and have the same attention and focous, you will find that this two sexes which you had yesterday and today are the same. If you have hundreds or thousands time this kind of sex with full attention, you can find that all of them are the same, so one is equal to thousand.

I have a suggestion:

When you go to a forest or sea, without thinking about anything else, focous on them.

Look at the height of the trees, the color of the leaves, breath deeply the fresh air and feel its coldness and pleasant feeling that you have after breathing. Touch the leaves, the trees, bushes and wet soils which are under your and tree's feet.

Touch the flowers, feel the softness of the flowers, look at their colors such a way that you never looked at them before. Talk to them and say to the flowers, how beautiful are they! Look at the grasses, touch them.

Listen to the forest's voices.

The birds, the stream of water or the voice of the waterfall if there is near you.

If you have a different attention than before, you can discover many new things. If you look, hear, touch and smell with more attention and repeat this actions and feelings in the next weeks or monthes, you will find that one is equal to thousand, so if one of your friend suggest you to go to forest, you can fully and completely feel all the joys and happiness which the forest can give you during the time that you are there. If you had felt the coolness, freshness, colors and other joyful feelings of the forest before, So you can undrestand that this time will be the same as weeks ago and if you can not go with your friends, you will never be sad because you felt the forest's environment completely and felt it by your all cells, but if you didn't have attention to the feelings which the forest could give to you in the pre – weeks, again you are not aware of where are you going and for what kind of feelings you are going to the forest.

From the morning

Most of us mention the morning as the beginning of our daily Life.

If you attention to your daily acts, you can find that most of your actions are repeating day after day.

You take a shower or wash your face after waking up and eat your breakfast.

You put on your clothes and shoes every morning and then go at your work by your own car, bus or subway.

You do your daily work as a clerk, business man teacher or etc.

After doing your job, you will back to your home.

When you back to your home after your daily work, some of you do hobbies. For example go to gym, pool, music institute, reading book or any thing that cause you spend your time and then go to your bed to spend one more night in your life and then wake up in the next morning. these repeatations are exhausting. Most of the poeple because of these repeatations in their life are depressed so some of these depressions causes to soicide or leaving the home or causes divorce in some families.

I have a suggestion:

Let's suppose that our life will beggin after a long night sleeping.

Before I say my suggestion, let me ask you a question.

Was it possible do not wake up in the morning and last night became your last time of sleeping in your bed?

If you think in a logical way and share rationality to your thinking, it is obvious that today or tonight can be our last day or last night for living. we can see this kind of thinking in two aspects.

The first one it is that we should thanks God who gave another chence to us for living one more day and we have another chance to take a shower, eat breakfast, go at work, back to our home and pass our time by our favorit hobbies.

In another aspect we can say that this morning or this day is our last day in this world and we will not be in thid world tomarrow. I ask you another question.

Can't it be your last day for living in this world?

It is obvious that today can be your last day of living. You can not guarantee that you will be alive tomorrow. Some of you may say that we can not guarantee that we can live even some minutes or some seconds later. Yes, you are right.

There is not any exception for anybody to live as long as she or he wants.

Nothing can stop the death that comes to you.

You can not say I will live a long time because I am young and God is too kind or I married recently and I have a little girl or boy and God is not so cruel to destroy my new life and God will never let my young wife become widow in her early mothering time.

There is not any guarantee.

So rationality shows that one day we should put down every thing we have in our life and leave them all.

You should leave your parents, wife, husband, friends, children, car, house, company and everything you have in your life.

Five sense s truggle

Please look at your environment, look at the people who are around you. You can see that most of them are working hardly and some time treat each other in a cruel way just for satisfy their five senses.

Don't go too far, just look at yourself or one person in your family.

We work to gain money to buy fruits in different colors and delicious foods just to satify the sense of tasting in ourselves.

You spend more time at work to gain more money to satisfy your hearing sense by buying some advance sterio or CD driver in your car or some eco instruments for your home, or you spend more mony to go some where like forests to hear the voice of birds, water falls or water streams.

You spend too time and money to satisfy your sight sense by going to the nature, sea, beautiful vallies or villages or buying TV to watch it or you buy camera to make a memory when you were in some beautiful memorable places and buy Computer or Lap top to watch your recorded clips or photos.

You spend too much time and money to build a house and buy a beautiful and soft bed to satisfy your sense of feeling. Some times you go to pool, sea, or buy soft shirts and clothes to satisfy your sense of feeling.

You spend too much time and money to buy your favorit perfum, your favorit flower or go to a far distance to be in a sea shore and smell a sea breeze. You do all these to satisfy your smelling sense.

So, you spend too much money and time to satisfy your five senses.

If you remember my words in the previous pages, I said that one is equal to thousand.

I'm not here to say that enjoying by your five senses is unacceptable or out of rationality, on the contrary I suggest you live with your five senses fully. Try to live with your five senses as much as you can.

Eat, watch, hear, smell and touch every thing or every one more and more and more.

Don't hesitate, don't delay your desires.

Don't say I will do, test, taste, touch, feel, smell, eat, watch, look, hear, listen or enjoy in the next time or even don't delay this enjoyments minutes or seconds.

Don't hesitate and don't delay because today may be your last day in your life as we talked about that befor.

If you live by your five senses many times and live with them fully, I will teach you a magical action that can change your life and will put you in a golden road for ever.

Of course it is very dangerous.

It is right that you can put your feet in the golden road but it can cause some people put their feet in the road of suicide.

Now I am going to show you how you can go to the golden road.

Befor this golden road, you should do some thing. You are not forced to do any new works or actions, you should live your life as usual. For better action we beggin our usual life from the morning but in a different way.

In The morning

A new day. You open the eyes and will see that you are alive. It is the most important part of our action because if you are not alive, you can not continue next actions. So, thanks God for one more chance to live in this world and enjoy from every things you have or you will have today.

Go to take a shower! you may ask why I should take a shower, I can wash my face and go for breakfast. My dear freind! If this morning be your last morning of your life, why you lose the chance of a nice shower? Feel the water when touches your skin. feel the water which drop on your head and face .When the water touches your body feel its warmness in the winter and coolness in the summer . Smell the soap or shampoo that you use for washing your head and body. feel how much smoothy and soft is soap and shampoo's lather.

Feel the lather and foam when you touch by your hands and rub it on your body and face. One more time feel the warm or cool water that spreads on your body from the shower. Feel it completely. Don't think any thing. Just concentrate and focous all your feeling on the water, spray of the shower, soap and shampoo's lather and enjoy from it fully, because you can not do any thing just taking the shower in this time. After washing your body, it is the time to feel a soft and dry towel on your skin. Feel completely the softness of towel.

Did you feel the softness of it after the shower? So I suggest you try it this morning. It is the time to wear your underwear after drying your body.

This days all underwears are made of very soft and nice garments and materials.

Feel it's softness and comfortness of your clothes too.

After a shower with using several senses, it is the breakfast time.

I ask you a question.

what will you eat for breakfast if it is your last brakfast in your life?

I know, If there is a little brain in your head you will chose and eat your favorite breakfast or at least you will eat the best one that you have at your home in this time.

Put things on the table in the best decorative and

artistic way that you can. Sit like a king and eat what you have on the table kingly. Eat slowly, have a complete attention to the tastes of every thing you eat. Focus on their tastes. Is it sweet? Is it Sour ? Is it salty? look at their colors. What color is the jam? what color is the bread? Smell the coffee! Smell the tea! Feel their pleasant warmness! Just focus on thier smells, color and tastes.

After a royal and pleasant breakfast, it is the time to go at your work.

when you are walking in the street, walk gently and don't be in a hurry. Look at every thing which are in your enviroment.

Look at the poeple, listen the bird's voice, look at the fresh trees. If it is winter, look at the snow and feel them when you put your feet on it. If it is a rainy day, listen the rain's voice when they fall on your umbrella.

If you are going by your own car, listen to your favorit music and enjoy your driving.

If you use public transportation, look at the poeple as you are smiling and sit down gently, like a king or queen.

Untransferable experience

when you lost something which appreciated it too much and then you see that others have the same thing that you didn't consider it important, they don't consider it important too, you will have a great sorrow.

when you want to tell them that hold and care this properties and try not to lose them, they just gaze at you and don't understand any thing.

Here is the point which you will understand that you can't transfer your experience.

you should wait and see, they experince by themselves.

You should let them to grow up themselves.

If you talk about your experience in religion, politic or life and they are not agree with you then you should let them to experience what you experienced.

Time will show the people what is right and what is wrong?

Don't challenge on things that needs time to be learned. Let the time to be passed and then you will find that you can transfer some experiences. Passing the time is the best teacher.

you should just see and suffer.

You are too rich

If you take a paper and pencil and try to write the name of each property that you have, you can write fifty or hundered of the things you have. For example: you may write, car, shoes, shirt, socks, bag, house, TV, radio, sofa, phone, etc. you can see that you continusly can write the things that you have. But, if you try to write things that you don't have, you can not writ more than five item. You may write more money for example. It shows that you have money, but you want more. So, money is not the thing that you don't have. If you look at your life, you can see that you are really rich. you have children, mother, father, friends, housband, wife and too many things which you can not put a price on it. So you are very rich. You are not poor. You just want some more. If you want some more, you should ask yourself what are you going to do by more? For example you have a car and you want one more car. What are you going to do with extra car? Is it necessary? Is it necessary to pay more money and spend more time to gain more money to pay for one extra car? So, you are rich. You should have more thing if it is realy necessary. This necessity belongs to all things that you have in your life.

Being a witness

Don't worry! Take it easy!
When some thing is going to happen, it will happen. Never mind you are there or you are not there. What is going to happen, it will happen. When a lion is going to hunt a calf in Africa, it doesn't matter you are there or not, anyway the lion will kill the calf. When an accident happened in the street and a child was killed, no matter if you were there or not. When one of your parents, your wife or husband or your child infected by an incurable disease he or she will die if you are near them or you are some where. If it is spring, the trees will blossom . you can not stop it or force it to do sooner than it's real time. When it is winter and the snow may destroy some building's roof or the road, you can not stop the snowing or the raining. There are too many things in the world or your enviroment that you can not change them. So what should we do? Many of this events may be very effective on your life. It may cause stress, or a very strong depression. We know that too many events happened befor

our life(before our birth)and will happen after our life (after our death). The life and living had continue in the past and will continue in the long future. When some thing is going to happen and you can not stop it, the only way it is to be as a witness. Just watch it as a witness and don't judge or interprate it. There is a great beautiful rule in the world". Every thing or event will be passed, if it is good or bad".

When you are in a happy place, it will be finished and the enjoing time will be passed. It is obvious that bad and unhappy times will pass and you will come out of that situation. Maybe some events have too strong effect which it may remain for weaks or months.

When you learned to be as a witness for each short good or bad events, it will help you to be witness for a long time effective events and overcome the problems.

For example when your father died, you can be as a witness in his funeral ceremony.

Just look at the people, the coffine, the tomb and the buriel act.

You should whatch yourself and the people as a third person. You can imagine yourself ten meter over the cemetry and watch the people, your father's coffine and yourself whom are in the crowd of people near the tomb.

Just watch every thing which is happening. It is very painful but you know that it will be finished one or two hours later.

You can see as a witness that there are some people near yourself that their father has dide in the past and it shows that you are not the only person who has lost his or her father. Those who their fathers are alive, they will lose their father in the near or far future. So you will logically accept this events. You can see some children that their father died many years ago and you can see that they are living as usual as other children who are living with their father.

When you are witness of yourself and your life, by watching the events, you will decide logically about things which you are going to manage them. When you are witness of your life, it is just like a person is watching your life second by second from a near dis tance and consulting with you after each event and takes a logical decision for your action.

Being a witness is not just for bad or sad events, as I said befor, it is for all of your actions and events which happen every second in your life during the 24hours, seven weaks, twelve months and as much as years that you live in this life. Being aware of your actions and thoughts is meditation.

Our voice or others voice

Every one hears and watches many things every day. We hear someone advices us or just talks to us or recomends us somethings.

The words which comes out of his or her mouth, sometimes it is his words and sometimes he borrowed the words from others.

If you do as he says, you are copying his life or you are continuing his life.

We should know that we are a unique creature. Every one has it's own life.

If you want to copy someone's life, you are wasting your life.

If you want to copy someone's life, you should be completely sure that you like and you enjoy to continue his way of living.

you should be sure if for example today is your last day for living, you are not regretful by doing that advices or recomendation and you are not regretful by passing your last days of your life by doing that job or act.

If you remember, I said before in this book that this minutes maybe our last minutes of living in this planet. So if it is your last day or last minutes of your life in this world, what will you do? will you copy others life and will you do what others said? Or you will do what is in your heart and in your desires? will you do exactly as the prescriptions that others wrote for you or you will do things that you like to do them?

So it's better to hear your inner voice which comes out from your heart.

In our ordinary life, you can see that many poeple, organization, institutes and groups plan for ourselves.

They plan and manage for us and say how and what should we eat? Where should we go? What should we wear? what is good to do? what is not suitable for us? how should we worship God? And too many orders which they write for us as rules like a prescription and they will punish you if you don't act exactly like their prescriptions .

Our parents are the first group that give us some rules step by step in order to control us and grow up us in such a way to make us a perfect man.

If you like to eat your food on the kitchen's floor instead of eating at the table, you will be confronted with an unpleasant reaction by your parents.If you insist to do what you want, you will be known as a rebelion for them.

We have a chance to live just one time in this world. We come to this world and then we leave here. This coming and leaving seems less than one hour or one minute.

All of us should remember that we will live just one time in this planet, we just live one time in this life, just one time, just one time and this chance of living will never be offered to you again.

After billion billion billion years you had the chane to come to this world and live here and after leaving this world you will never have the permision to come again and the mos t dramatic point it is that today may be your last day of this great and rare chance. So live as perfect as you can!

Let others think that you are a rebelion . It is obvios that nobody in his last day of living do a wrong thing or do things that hurt others, because he don't have spare time for others, so don't listen to other's voice. Just listen to your heart and do what you want becouse you don't have enough time and you don't have second chance to live in this planet and this world again.

Time travel

Every body can have time traveling. If you ask some one, can you go to past time ? can you go to repeat som thing that happened in the past? You may hear that " it is impossible". But I can say it is possible and all people can do that. Every body did it hundred times.

If you ask someone , what are you doing this day? She or he will answer "nothing , I just do the things as usual".

You go every day at work, you beggin your job at 8 o'clock and finish it at 2 or 4 pm. What does it mean? It doesen't show you that, you do a work, the same acts every day? It doesen't mean that, it's like you go to past time to do and repeat the acts wich you did past days?

How many acts do you know that you repeat everyday or every weeks?

When you are not satisfied by doing your job in past days, you can change your behavior or way of acts to be satisfied. It shows that you could be able to go to the past time and corect one of your faults. So I ask you again, is time travel possible?

Yes, you are right , we can not have time traveling in many cases, but as I told before , it is not impossible. So, look at yourself. look at your inner acts or behaviors like, anger, kindness , happiness, jelosy and etc, and look at your acts which happens in your environment like doing your job, greetings asking something, buying and ect. If you did something in the past and it bothers you, and you want to compense, you can do time travelling and meet the same person or same place and cause to create the same situation and by repeating that act, with a different decision you can have a different result. So the satisfaction comes to you.

When we can do a time travelling and changing our inner feeling, so why we regret to do this action? Maybe today is our last day for living in this world or may be this minutes are the last minutes for living in this planet. So travel to the past and cpmpense some acts or travel to the future by giving something or telling some words which you want to give or tell some one ten or twenty years later.

How can I be a mystic?

Mysticism has just one message.If you obey this message and spend all of your life time around this message,you will be a mystic person. you may ask : what is that message?

This message says: love, love and love all animals, plants, things and human being without expecting any rewards or action in return.

If you want to be a mystic you should be a pure lover and if you want to be a pure lover, you should not have any desire or will. If you live fully and completely, you will never have any desire.

When you use all your senses and be satisfied by using them and nothing can satisfy you, it's the time of being a mystic. You may ask how can I don't have any desire? When you use all your senses every time and every day, you will come to a point that no foods, no views, no voices, no drinks and I should better to say that really nothing can satisfy you.

Because you know the taste of all foods , all drinks

and you saw many beautiful places, weard many beautiful clothes and you had too many times sex with beautiful women . When comes a time that you don't enjoy from anythings, you will have two decisions. The first decision is to doing suicide because there is not anything to satisfy you and enjoy it.

The second decision it is to find different things that you can enjoy from them.

Now it's the time of borning a new mystic.

When you can not enjoy by your five senses, you should go beyond five senses and do some thing that increase energy and joy in yourself.

When you help an old man or woman who is car-rying a heavy thing, you feel a kind of joy that you can't feel it by your five senses, so kindness, love, helping, empathy, and this kinds of feelings can sat-ify you and will become a great cause for you to continue your life in a beautiful and atractive way. Mystics are those who just enjoy from love and love.

Children

Our children will be born the same as we were born years ago. The brith of our children is the cycle of our life, they will be born, grow up, will become a young man or woman and they will be an old person and then they will leave this world the same as us, our fathers and mothers. If you wanted to be free in your chilhood, let your children be free. If you want to test every thing around you and experience them, so let your children to experience what they want. If you want to have a powerful, genius, kind, happy and a great child, please go away from their way . I want to repeat it. Please go away from their way. Let them to be themselves. They are not your property. You just had a sex one night in the bed and then this child camed to your life and you say this little human being is mine. Shut up please!

Just put them free and do what you can do for them by love and kindness. Respect them. Respect their decisions. Respect them as you expected your parents do for you.

When children are growing up,they always are thinking about the things and events in their environment but when they are young, they stop thinking and just imitate. A person can grow up untill he thinks.when a person stops thinking, he will stop growing up. So don't let them to imitate. let them be themselves. If they do something wrong, they will have experience and they will find by themselves that it was wrong. And experience will expand their views to the life. There is not different between girls and boys. The only difference is in their apearance. Their soul is the same. The environment which they are living is the same. The foods which they are eating are the same, their education is the same, their gens are the same, they can do the same job, they can have the same hoby, so they are not different from each other, they have one difference and that is their sex organs. When they share their sex this difference complete each other and again they becom the same, because they enjoy the same thing and they have the same feeling during the sex.

A golden rule

Every body should know that nobody can help you exept yourself. If you think a little, you will find that when you have a problem in your life and refer to a physition, lawyer, psycologist, one of your friends or some one in your family, it is obvious that they just can shair some minutes of their times with you and they can't leave their home and always stay with you, because they have their own life.

You should know that you, yourselves are the writer, player and director of your life. Every one has his own problem. If you want to have a better life, you should solve ninety percent of your problem, yourselves.

If you have not enough money, you should find a job and work harder. Nobody can help you whole your life time.

If you are not happy enough and you feel depression, nobody can come and stay with you forever to make you happy.

There are just two ways. The first one it is that you

can stay poor and depressed or you may choose the second way to earn more money by working harder and make your life full of joy.

If you want to have a happy life, you should work , buy good foods and clothes, live in a clean place , go to a trip, have a weakly or monthly party and help others by your money or your kindness and love.

Those who are happy and have a high quality life, they just do things which I told you in the last paragraph.

Nobody knows

Who knows where is he or she from?
Nobody knows where he or she was before his birth.
Nobody knows why she is a woman or he is a man.
Nobody knows why some people live shorter than others or why some people are richer.
Are those long life people or rich one, different creatures for creator of this world?
Nobody knows, is there justice or not?
Nobody knows why people die exactly in their wedding day.
Nobody knows why some people didn't see their child when their wife was pregnant because he died before his child's birth.
Nobody knows why some people who are cruel gain money easier than kind and generous one.
Nobody knows why some children in some countries work hard and never go to school but some children in some countries have the best facilities and never work before finishing their school.
Nobody knows why some people were killed in

some countries because of their idea and believes.
How long is a man or woman's life?

Human being before twenty is just experiencing the
unknown world and society which he or she was
born in it.

After twenty he will find that for living in this world
should have a job and should have income.

He tries to be a rich man, to have a luxury life. He
experiences several business and meets different
people in his life. If he become successful and be
able to be a rich man, he will pass twenty or thirty
years to have a good financial situation, so he is
about fifty years old.

A young man in order to be a rich man should pass
many stressful times and situations, so he is not
healthy enough.

These kind of people who had stressful business can
not have long life. If they are lucky may live until
seventy.

So between fifty years old which he become a rich
man in this age and seventy years old, he just can
live twenty years as a sick rich man.

Nobody knows why a man works too hard and harms
himself and others, to become just a rich man.

Nobody knows that he or she just has one life and
it is not obvious that when this life will be ended.

Some people think that their life has two parts. In the first part he should work and in the second part he should live.

But experience shows that there is not guarantee for anyone to live one minute more.

So I don't know how some people split their life time into two parts. The first part just working and working and the second part resting and enjoying from their saved wealth.

Nobody knows how long he will live. How he can see his life in this way and divide his life from wealth to death?

Nobody knows is it a chance that some children born in poor or rich country? Is their fate? Who selects this fate for them?

Nobody knows why we be born in a country or land which we can't select it and we can't determine our life time.

We should struggle for existence if we be born in a poor or dictatorship country. If we try to be rich in these kind countries or exterminate the dictator leader, we will waste our life just for money and freedom. We have just one life and we will die anyway.

Nobody knows who and how should answer the question of those who never meet even a normal life and left this world by suffering, pain, annoyance, hopelessness, grief and trouble.

Nobody knows why the creator of this world don't care his creations?

Nobody knows is there any creator? Is he alive?

Is he watching this world? Can he control the events? Or he just created this world and then he died.

Nobody knows is the creator the created?

Did the creator devote himself to this world and is he part of this world? Is he himself whole or part of this world which he don't has any self-will to control it?

Nobody knows, has he the self-will or he granted the will to the creatures?

Nobody knows what will happen after the death. Religion says that there is a world different from our world which we are living now. The world of religion, after the death has two parts. One part for good people, its name is heaven and one part for bad people that its name is hell.

But scientists say that there is not any different between human and other creatures.

They say; human, animals, plants and other substances which are in this world, all are the same, all have same source, all are a form of energy, all are made of substances which comes from one origin.

So these substances make different things with different quality. These substances have a fixed quantity and have the ability to turn to energy and in another reaction the energy can be turn to substance. The amount or quantity of the substances and energy never change and always have a fixed amount.

Scientists say that turning the substances to energy and energy to substances includes all the world and universe.

Acording to scientists, a tree or any plant after cutting and falling down begins to decompose and disintegrating. All of his substances will return to the nature. Its water and minerals will back to the soil and some gases which produces during the disintegrating will back to the atmosphere. So this plant will never grow again. If you see some plants similar to the dead plant, they are just similar to it and non of them is exactly the same plant.

If you see the animal's life according to this theory , you can see when an animal for example a lion dies, its body begins to disintegrating and after a while its body turns to the environment substances. Lion's body will turn to minerals, gases and water or steam. You will never see the dead lion again. If you can see some lions, they are just similar to dead lion.

Scientists say that human as we said before has the same origin and substances like plants and animals. When a plant dies and can't back to the earth as itself or when an animal dies and can't back to the world as the same and like itself, the human is like them and according to this, when a person dies, he will never back to the world.

A person was not in this world before his birth. The universe was billion years turning and turning but the person was not in this world. He don't know where he was.

He can't remember even one second of pre-birth's world or situation. He comes to this world and if we take an average, he may live eighty years (as we know this time for living in comparison with the time of creation of the universe is les than a blink) in this world.

After a short life he will die and will never back between us.

Where he goes? How will be his life? Is he happy or sad?

According to scientists, he didn't go anywhere. He is here on the earth.

Before his birth he was just some substances. These substance become ovule and semen.

After a while it will become sperm and step by step by receiving mor substances from his mother's body , the little sperm grows up and after nine months it will be a baby.

This baby use the substances of his environment as foods. Som substances turn to food and his baby uses these foods.

He will live and live then he will die by accident, cancer, war and etc.

After the death, his body will breakdown and be disintegrated. When his body's substances back to the nature, he is not in this world, the same as his pre-birth time.

Before his birth, the world was turninig and turning for billion years. After his death, the world will turning and turning for billion years.

Nobody knows who is right? The religion or science.

Depression

Human lives with his acts. If you don't have any act or things for doing, you are dead. A child plays with his or her toys, a student studies his lessons, some people go at work, some people have hobbies and etc. So, you can see every one has some thing to do. A person will die when has nothing to do or do a routine act.

When you don't have any hobby or job to do, you will think that you are useless and you will be depressed.

When you do a routine job or act the same as jobless people you will be depressed too.

When you feel depression, it shows that you don't have any thing to do. It shows that you are not doing anything or you are doing a routine action. So, when you feel depression, try to experience a new thing in your life. Make a change in your life. Sometimes a small change may cause a great result.

Sometimes going out for walking cause a great change in your feeling that you can not believe it.

When I say experience, it doesn't mean to do expensive hobbies.

When you are unhappy and depressed, just change your position or do a new act or experience things, places or hobbies which you didn't experience before.

Wealth

What do you think about wealth? What is wealth?
Is it money? Is it a big and luxury house? Is it a factory?
Some people may think in spiritual way. Some people may say that the ability to help poor people or love the animals is the real wealth. Some people may say that a heart full of love is the real wealth. You may say, if you don't have money, how can you help poor people?
Wealth is what you can use it. You may have too many things, but you use some of them, so the extra things which are not in use, they are not wealth.
If you have three cars and just use one car, just this one is your wealth. That two cars are your property , not your wealth.
Wealth gives you happiness, aliveness, soulfullness succulence, pleasance and joy. Property gives you anxiety and you are concern about it. When you have ten cups and drink in one of them and enjoy by drinking in it and enjoy watching it, this cup is your

wealth and those nine extra cups are your property. Just one cup gives you joy and happiness then you are using it and you are concern about that nine cups because they may be broken or may be stolen.

This way of thinking works for every things, even for your heart.

If your heart gives you happiness by loving other creatures, it is your wealth. When your heart is always worried about others may ask you something and is concern about paying money to poor people, this kind of heart is not your wealth, it is your property. Wealth gives you happiness and joy but property gives you worriment and concerns you.

The lost life

What are we doing these dayes?

Is this the real life? Is this the life that we are born to pass our life time?

What should we do?

What should not we do?

What does impact on our life?

Our family? The society? The government?

The religion?

What is our role?

Should we obey all of them?

If we obey them, who will be the successful?

Our family want to gain their lost hopes and lost goals as they lost in their life, by their children.

The governments want to show that the people belive them and obey their political program.

The religious groups want to show that they have more fans than other religions.

Those who control the society wants to show you that you are a humble citizen to achive their most ultimate benefits. Are you happy between them or you are waisting your short precious life time?

Don't waist and don't lose your life for things that different groups struggle together on it and each group or union tries to tell that they are right and rejects other groups.

If you open your eyes and your mind, the right opinion , idea or correct way , will show itself to you.

Don't waist your time by joining to political, socials or religious groups. Just be honest and obey your heart. Our creator have put a strong and accurate instrument in our heart to judje and scale everythings which seems very difficult to be distinguished.

Far from your body brings enlightenment

when you know yourself, you can know your environment and then world. Knowing yourself is the
first step to be enlighted and become a mystic.
If you want to know yourself you should separate
yourself into two parts.
The first part is your five senses. You should live
fully in your five senses as you feel that there is not
any desire for you to do by your five senses. You
should live In your five senses such a way that you
become disappointed and want to suicide. If you
look at billionair's life, you can see that they have
highest range of suicide, because they feed their five
senses and they don't know anything else to enjoy
it.
Those who want do suicide, just have one step to be
a mystic. If you know a mystic or an enlightened person in your environment and ask them, you will find
that they have reached to a moment in their life that
they should do suicide but they did it in a different

way.

When you enjoyed and did every thing in your life and don't have any desire, will or even very small thing to do, it's the time of suicide.

But now is the time to go a little far from yourself. When you don't enjoy by eating food, you can give your food or buy food for a little girl or boy or an old man or woman whom needs some thing to eat and that time you feel something which is more joyful than eating that food yourself. When you don't enjoy from sex, you will look at the women and girl in a different way. Your eyes don't slides on their body. You just look at their beauty, their kindness, their lovely behavior and you will discover some beauties that you have never seen before and you will enjoy when you spend time with them more than sex.

When you help an old woman or when you go to an asylum , a nursing home or charities and help some disable people, you will enjoy and feel something that you can not express by words. You feel that you are drunk. You feel drunk such a way that no kinds of drinks can do it.

When you enjoy by helping others in any way, you will reach to a golden word and that golden word is "love". Love means give others what you can without expecting any return.

No matter what are you going to give or devote. It can be a smile to a person in the morning when you are going at work, or it can be sharing your sandwich to your friend or someone who you don't know him or her. You can say hello to birds, cats and children. You can smile to flowers and touch them. You can hug the tress and kiss them.

You can sit near an old woman or man in the park and spend some minutes with them and drink some fruit juice together. You can help your wife at home and help her in cooking and washing, going to meet your parents, brother or sister.

So love every one and every thing. Life is short. When you passed your first part, it's the time to suicide and entering the second part and that is love. Your first part as I told you before is your five senses and your second part is love. When your life surrounded with love, you are an enlighted person and you have reache to enlightenment and you are a mystic.

An enlighted person or a mystic looks the world as it is. He enjoys what happens to him or her. Because he has decided to kill himself but now he learned how to enjoy in this world. If some unpleasant things happens, never mind, because this disaster is not worse than death. Every morning we have a new chance to live one day more, so love every plants, animals, insects, things and people. Never mind if they love you or not.

How can we be a billionair?

Some person prefer to have as much as is sufficient for their daily life. So they do their normal work and by their usual wage are very satisfied. Some people want to have more money to live the same as rich people and enjoy like them.

It is obvious that if you want to have more money you should work more harder and have some invention in your life to expand your business and it takes more time and energy.

Before you decide to be a billionaire, you should ask a question from yourself.

Do you want to gain money jus t like the billionair or you want to enjoy your life just like the billionair and rich people? You want to have more money to do what?

If you ask this question from yourself you may give several answer to yourself.

You may say I want more money to buy a big house. If you have a big house you may spend ten hours each day at your home and sleep eight hours in your bed room.

If you have twenty bed room, you should go to sleep just in one bedroom, so it is obvious that you need one bedroom not more. A billionaire person just can sleep in one bedroom and can sleep in one bed, but he may have very comfortable and luxury bed. So if you be able to buy a comfortable and luxury bed, you can spend at least eight hours of your daily life exactly like a billionair because your sleeping condition is the same. If you comfort your bedroom as comfort as a billionair's bedroom, one third of your life time is the same.

Before I explain this case, I should remember you a rule about pleasure and enjoyment.

One is equal to thousand. What does it mean?

For example, If you drink apple juice for first time, its taste is the same as second, third or even thousandth time. Taste of a food in first time is the same as eating it thousandth.

Sex in tenth time is not more joyful than the second time, or hundredth time is not more joyful than tenth time and it is the same for thousandth time.

So, we can say that one is equal to thousand.

Now we are going to answer our main question. What do you want to do, if you become a billionair? I told you about house of a rich man. Its bedroom and the time he or she spends in it as a place for rest. Many people try too much to gain more and more money but they don't know what is their goal or goals. They just buy house, car and go to luxury and beautiful places.

A rich man spends too much money to buy a very expensive house just because to sit on a chair in its balchony which has a view to the sea and drink a cup of tea or coffee and smoke a cigarette when he or she is looking at the sea and its beach just three days a year, because he don't have enough time to enjoy from this place and he should go to continue his business and if he had enough time, some months later will go to his another house in another country or city.

If you go to a hotel and sitdown in its blachony which has the same view of the expensive house which we have talked before and drink tea or coffee and look at the sea and its beach, what's the different between you and that rich man who is seating and looking at the same view and drinks just like you?

I want to give you another example. Suppose a rich man has fifteen cars. Can he use all of his cars in the same time? It is obvious that if he wants to go out, he should use just one car. When he is in the road is seating on one car not in fifteen cars and you are seating in one car the same as the rich man. If you want to have diversity in using the different cars. You can change using the different cars, you can change it every year and enjoy from different brands, like a rich man.

I have told you before that in enjoyment, one is equal to thousand.

When you go to a five star hotel and stay one or two night in it, you can use and enjoy from all its facility and be conscious when you look, touch or taste every thing in this hotel. When you could feel and use and enjoy from all facilities, it will be the same if you go to five star hotels ten times or hundreds. When you go to five star hotel one time, you will know how is its bed quality or how is its foods taste.

You should remember that rich people don't have enough time to enjoy from their money. Average-income people enjoy more than rich people. If you do or use the things that rich people do or use, just one time by consciousness, there is not any difference between you and rich people.

«Try to use properly what you have in your life».

When you are drinking a cup of tea, drink it like a king. Use a beautiful cup, sit in a silent place, smell the tea and drink it gently and joyfully. I promis nitynine percent of rich people never drink a cup of tea the same as I described now. They may use expensive cups but they are not aware of drinking tea or water.

They have a very busy mind and their body and soul are not balanced.

My theory

Most of the people specially those who have religious believes, deeply believe that God created all these creatures separately one by one and gives his soul to them for a short period and then this soul will return to God and will experience a different situation or condition which will be separated to hell and heaven.

I am not here to reject this believe. I just want to say what is my own view to the world and its creatures. I want to say my view about soul and its connection to all creatures. Before I explain briefly my theory, I should give you an example which is very touchable for you.

We know that there are different kinds of waves in our environment. We use this waves for radio, satellite, internet or phone communication. Maybe there are some different waves which have secret usage and ordinary people like us have not permission to connect to them to use it.

For using each wave we need its special device. For

example if we want to use the waves which cause to have voice communication or text communication, we should have the special device like cell phone.

Some cell phones have the ability to use waves just for voice or text communication, so does it mean there is not more waves in our environment? Exactly, No!

There are different kinds of waves which need their special device to change them to information.

Each device has its special ability and according to its inner components will be more advanced than others. When you use an ordinary cell phone and just take voice or text message it doesn't mean that there is not more information in your environment, as I told before, you just need an advanced device to receive more information.

You can use an advanced device to have picture, video and internet information more than voice and text messages.

Even may be there are more waves which can be processed to very important information but we need its special device which they may are under the control of security or army services.

I don't want to write about security services or things like these. I just want you to know that each information needs its special device to be processed and become useful for someone or somethings.

Now, I am going to tell you more about my theory.

Every body heard the word "soul", but each person has its own view to the soul according to his or her religious learning.

This world is made of things which we can see and we can not see. The things which we can not see, has surrounded every thing. It surrounded the earth and everythings which are on it, the moon, all stars, planets and it's better to say the all universe.

This unseen things may be called enerjy, soul or any thing that you like, but I want to call it "information". Acording to my idea, the universe surrounded by information. This information is wise, is talented, genius and has curiosity. this information is unlimited. As you can't count and say the number of stars in the universe, you can not estimate or say about the information too. This information is about chemistry, physics, philosophy, biology, mathematic, sociology, astrology, psychology and everythings which you can think about it.

In order to gain this information from our environment we should have the prope device and each device has its own capacity and ability to gain this information from its environment and process it for itself to use it.

Plants like trees have their special device. They just can gain some information by their devices to learn how make fruit. Their device just help them to gain information and learn how lose their leaves and how have leaf and blossom in spring. Their device gain some information and process it and cause the tree to learn how be alive in cold winter when it is naked and without any cover.

But animals are more advanced than plants, because their devices which makes their body are more advanced and complicated than plants. So they can process more information and can use more complicated information.

In compare with plants. Animals can move, run, jump, eat, scape from dangers and sometimes they can decision on simple situation.

Why trees don't shake their branches voluntarily when they confronted with danger?

We know there is an information which can tell us If you shake the branches you can keep away the danger. Why the tree don't use this information? It is obvious that the tree doesn't have the proper device to gain this information and process it.

What about human being? Human has brain. The brain is the most powerful device which has been known in this world. The brain can process the information which surrounded our environment. This brain even can process the body's information like blood pressure, shortage of some vitamins and then can make a decision to protect it from some diseases. It should be said that the brain as a device differs from one person to another one.

One person can take more information from his environment and process it better and then use it in a proper situation for more benefition, but another person in the same position and place may not be able to gain and process the same information. It shows that one brain is a little more advanced than another one.

For example Anistain and his classmate are thinking on a phisics problem. Why Anistain solves the problem and his thinking cause to a theory but others don't do like him?

I should say that, the information which Ainstain could find it, was in all student's environment.

All students had the same opportunity to gain the information, so why others couldn't do that?

All of them have the same brain in shape, but if we mention the brain as a device, Ainstain's brain is a little more advanced than others.

I have wrote before that each creature has its own device and can by processing the information which surrounded him have relation to their environment by its device.

Plants, animals and human beings according to their device's capacity and ability can gain information and continue their life.

A tree, an animal's body and a human's body is a device. This information can be mentioned as "soul".

According to my idea each creature doesn't have its own soul. Each creature is connected to a great unic soul. The soul is like an ocean.

A fish doesn't have its own ocean. A fish is connected to the ocean.

A cell phone doesn't have its own waves.

A cell phone is connected to an ocean of waves. A creature doesn't have it's own soul.

A human doesn't have its own soul. A human is connected to an ocean of soul.

You may ask, what will happen to us after the death?

I ask you a question. What will happen to a cell phone when it ruind or demolished? Does the waves will be demolished or become changed to any thing else? It is obvious that when a cell phone or tablet go off, they are dead, they are useless but the communicative waves are in our environment the same as before. The waves are available and accessable.

A new cell phone can use the waves and process them, even

the new cell phone may be more advanced than before.

The body is the same. When a body dies, it just become disconnected to the ocian of information.

A new body will be born and will be connected to his environment's unlimited information.

Leader of a country

Who is the best leader of a country? When I say leader I mean president, king or a religious leader. When you are going to see who is the best leader of a country you should look at the output of the country. You should look at the output of human rights , the out put of economy, the output of freedom for media like newspaper, magazine, TV and the ability to critic the government and leadership in public.

When you put all of these politically, economically, socially and culturally together, you should find a positive and pessimistic out put.

When you see a group of leaders try to stop the war in a country and not only they can but also they make it worst and cause the people lose their home, their children and their family. It shows that these group of leaders don't have the ability for leadership.

A leader should be pessimistic and very sensitive.

A leader should think like a man and act like a woman.

Life is very short. If a leader destroys people's life to

make his power stronger, he will never have enough
time to make people's life again.

Walking like a king

You can wear your best clothes, your shiny shoes and prepare yourself for a kingly walking.

You can call your girl friend or manage with your wife or even you, yourself can go to a public garden and suppose that this garden belongs to you. You are the owner of this garden and walk like a king in your beautiful garden and suppose that you are generous enough to let others to use your garden and spend their time in your private property.

If you really were a king how often you had enough time to walk in your garden? Maybe once a week or twice a month , because you as a king didn't have enough time to have an every day walking in your garden. So you can go once a week or twice a month like a king to a public garden and walk there and look at your people and mention them as your guard or as whom you let them to walk with you in your garden.

When you go by taxi, you can image that this is your own car and you have your own driver.

When you eat your breakfast, eat the best food you like and spend more time to eat your breakfast or lunch kingly.

When you talk with your friends or some people, talk with them like a gentleman and behave kingly. Wear like a king, eat like a king, walk like a king, talk like a king and sleep in a very clean and well decorated bed like a king.

Every person has his own life time

When you look at your environment, you can see that all families send their children to school and then to university inorder to have a good life.

All parents think that their child will be graduated at 21 and then he or she will find a perfect job and then will buy house and car and will marry with a nice and beautiful girl and these young couple will have beautiful children.

I want to say some words to parents. How many people you know that they never went to university but they become very successful person?

Some people started their successful company when they passed 40.

Some people decided to go university when they were older than 30.

Some people found their suitable and lovely job when they passed 35.

Some people never finished their university but after some years they decided again to go university.

Some people married when they were very young

and less than 25 but after 20 years they don't have a child but some people married when they were more then 40 but they could have a child in their first year of marriage.

Some people become famous when they were less than 20 but some famous people never been known before their 60th.

Some people were very rich in their young time but they become very poor in their old time.

Some people were very poor in their young time but they become very rich in their old time.

We can see that every person has his or her own life time.

Don't blame those who are not successful or rich. You don't know what will happen for a person in near future.

Appreciate your child, your father, mother, sister and all the people whome are living in your environment.

You should always remember that every person has his or her own life time and nobody knows what will happen for others.

Bubble world

Did you see the bubbles? What is it made of?

Yes, a very thin cover of water like a dome and some air under this dome.

Where was this bubble before? Where does it go after bursting?

All we know that the materials which made the bubble are in this world.

These materials there were before making the bubble and they will be in this world after bursting and fading the bubble.

If we mention all of the creations in this world as a bubble, how can we see this world?

Look at a tree. We know that all trees which are in our environment there were not before. They were a seed, then they become a seeding and grew up then became a perfect tree. After some years or decades this tree will be broken and fall down or will become dried wood. The dried wood or better to say the dead tree will disintegrate and all of its materials which made its trunk will back to the nature the same as a bubble which was born, lived and then died or faded. When a bubble be born by a little water and air, nothing will increase to this planet and when this bubble bursts and fades nothing will decrease from this planet.

When a tree grows up nothing will increase and when it disintegrates nothing will decrease in this planet which we know it as "Earth".

The animals are the same as bubbles and trees. Animals will be born, live and then die.

The same as bubbles and trees which can't increase or decrease anything in this planet and in this world, the animals can't do any extra thing like them.

We can add human being to this group. Human being the same as bubbles, trees and animals will be born, live and then will be die.

All creatures has the same fate. All creatures will be born and then fade. Not only the bubbles, plants and human being, be born and then burst but also other planets and stars be born and then burst like a bubble.

So, we know that everything in this world (I mean earth, other planets, stars, galaxies and every thing which we can see or we can not see) has the bubble life.

The materials and energies never increase or decrease

but they turn from one shape to other shape.

For example a plant can be eaten by an animal and the plant turns to be meat in animal's body.

A bubble "plant" bursts or fades and another bubble "the animal" will be a little bigger and some day latter this bubble "animal" will be burst and will make another bubble (may be human being or other animal) a little bigger. You! yes. I mean exactly you that are reading this book, are a bubble too. You was born some years ago and will die some times latter. You were made by some materials the same as a bubble which has mad by its own materials and then will burst like the bubble of our story and finally the materials which you are mad of them, will return to the nature.

As a bubble was not in this world before its birth, you were not in this world too and as a bubble which bursts and fades after his life and never can come back again, you as a human being can not back to this world again.

If after bursting a bubble, you see another bubble, it is not the same bubble. It is just similar to that bubble.

This rule consists all trees, animals, human beings and all creatures of the world.

A bubble bursts then a similar one comes. A tree

falls down and another similar tree comes.

A man or woman dies and another similar man or woman comes.

Don't forget that we are living in a bubble world and we are one of these bubbles.

Unfortunately we don't know when our bubble will burst. It maybe today or some minutes later.

So, be aware and live consciously. Enjoy from eating, drinking, wearing your best clothes, walking, talking with you friends, talking with your parents, hugging your wife or children, driving your car or bycicle, watching the flowers and trees, feeding the animals, helping others, buying a gift for your friend or family, jump like a child on the grass, touch the soil or sands, take a shower and do hundreds more things.

Live without discipline

If you live by discipline, you will waste your life. Governments for governing on you, force you to live in discipline because if you live as you want, how can they be as a ruler and use your time and energy for their powerful and luxury life?

Be yourself! Do what you want! Go everywhere you like! Eat everything that you enjoy! If you do exactly as the rulers want, you will certainly waste your life. Don't lose your life! Just enjoy it because you have just one-time chance for living in this world and you will never come again to this planet.

I suggest you live without discipline and do what you want but you should remember a great rule. Don't disturb others for your freedom and enjoyment.

Immatured olds

I believe that the age of a person never proves his ability. You may saw some 60 or 80 years old people who are not as wise as they should be. Some old people are less experienced than some young who are less than 20.

You may saw that some teen boy or girls are matured than some old people.

Being a wise man never depends on some one's age. Being wise or matured is a quality which depends on some one's intelligence.

When someone has a curious and deep attention to his or her environment or the events which are happening in his family or society, he will seem more mature than his age and he will seem more mature than those who are older than him.

So oldness never proves that someone is matured and intellect enough to advise those who are younger. If you have more attention to your environment and be aware of your acts and saying, you can be more mature than others.

Never Forget! Today, may be your last day
for living in this world.